Theological Encyclopædia
> 16mo. Price, net, 35 cents

Sacerdotalism in the Nineteenth Century. A Critical History
> Crown 8vo. Gilt top. Price, net, $2.00

Unbelief in the Nineteenth Century. A Critical History
> Crown 8vo. Gilt top. Price, net, $2.00

History of Christian Doctrine
> Fourth Edition. Revised. 8vo, 2 volumes. Price, $3.50

System of Christian Doctrine
> 8vo. Price, $2.50

RUDOLF EUCKEN'S MESSAGE TO OUR AGE—AN APPRECIATION AND A CRITICISM

BY
HENRY C. SHELDON
Professor in Boston University

New York: EATON & MAINS
Cincinnati: JENNINGS & GRAHAM

Copyright, 1913, by
HENRY C. SHELDON

193
E864
S544r

PREFACE

It was with no thought of publication that the essay on the teaching of Rudolf Eucken was written. Only the plea that it would afford useful guidance to many who are asking what they ought to think of the system of the distinguished philosopher has led us to consent to have it placed before the public. We trust that the reader will notice the relatively large space which is given to an appreciative exposition, and will not allow the criticism which is passed upon some phases of Professor Eucken's theological thinking to stand in the way of a high valuation of his philosophy proper.

Boston University,
January, 1913.

I

Two main endeavors come to very emphatic manifestation in the writings of Rudolf Eucken, Professor of Philosophy in the University of Jena. On the one hand, he aims to uncover with utmost distinctness the great deficiencies of the age. On the other hand, he seeks to direct to the remedy which is alone adequate. Whatever may be the estimate of his success in his chosen task, no one can question the deeply earnest and religious spirit in which he has taken up and pursued that task.

Letting the Professor speak as far as possible for himself, we will forthwith illustrate his view on the characteristic deficits of the age by citing a few paragraphs from writings recently given to the public. In his book on The Truth of Religion he writes as follows:

"We witness with painful clearness

to-day a strong decline of inward culture; ever less does man find definite satisfaction in all the bustle of our modern mechanism; ever more is the inward life lowered in its pitch to the commonplace; and ever clearer it becomes apparent that all the gain on the periphery of life cannot counterbalance the loss which occurs at the center. In the last resort it is true that we live our existence from out the center, and, although this fact may be forgotten in our relationship to the environment, it can never be permanently lost. . . . It is an age afflicted with an immense contradiction. It is wonderfully great in its mastery of and achievements within the environing world; but, on the other hand, it is deplorably poor and insecure in regard to the problems of the inner life and the inner world."[1]

In another volume Professor Eucken remarks:

---

[1] Pp. 117, 118, 605.

"The position at the present moment conclusively proves that the content of man's life is not the easy, unsought product of a natural process of historical development, for, after all the weary work of many thousand years, we are to-day in a condition of painful uncertainty, a state of hopeless fluctuation, not merely with regard to individual questions, but also as to the general purpose and meaning of life."[1]

Again he observes:

"A paralyzing doubt saps the vitality of our age. We see a clear proof of this in the fact that, with all our astounding achievements, we are not really happy. There is no pervading sense of confidence and security, but rather a tendency to emphasize man's insignificance, and to think meanly of his position in the universe. A closer scrutiny reveals the presence of a

---

[1] The Problem of Human Life as Viewed by the Great Thinkers, p. 565.

genuine endeavor to unify life, but even so the processes adopted are so widely divergent as to be directly antagonistic. . . . Over against a lavish output of departmental work we have to set a woeful incapacity to deal with life as a whole, and a growing uncertainty as to the goal aimed at and the nature of the path to be followed."[1] "Sharp contrasts have always been found in human experience; and in transitional periods in history they have been felt with painful acuteness. But never did they so extend over the whole life and so deeply affect fundamentals; never was there so much uncertainty with regard to what should be the main direction and endeavor and the meaning of all human existence and man's relation, as in the present."[2]

If it is the office of a prophet not to utter smooth things, but to lay bare

---

[1] The Meaning and the Value of Life, p. 2.
[2] Life's Basis and Life's Ideal, pp. 93, 94.

the faults of the contemporary generation, then Eucken may be regarded as fulfilling somewhat of a prophetical vocation in his unsparing criticism of the present age. Over against the self-complacency and self-puffery in which the age is so prone to indulge, his message on its essential poverty as respects the deeper things of life may well provoke to serious reflection.

II

In reviewing the means for meeting the inward destitution or spiritual poverty of the time, Eucken emphasizes the futility of resorting to anything not as deep-reaching and fundamental as the lack itself. Among all the schemes which put forward their claims, he rates naturalism, or that scheme which construes man as a mere piece of nature, as the most unsatisfactory. It is without logical basis, being contradicted by the fact that in cognizing and interpreting nature man demonstrates that he is above its plane. "If our intellect were no more than naturalism can logically make it out to be, it could at most refine the animal presentations a little; it never could have advanced beyond the single presentations to a representative conception of the world as a whole. Such an advance can be achieved only by thought raising itself above the stream of appearances and placing itself over against it; but how could a mere bundle of perceptions, to which naturalism reduces the intellect, achieve this? Incomparably more unity of being and freedom of operation are necessary for this achievement than such a bundle could produce."[1] "Even the most zealous champion of nature cannot deny that we achieve something distinctive; we not only belong to nature, we have knowledge of the fact; and this knowledge is in itself sufficient to show that

---

[1] Life's Basis and Life's Ideal, p. 30.

we are more than nature."[1] While thus naturalism is superficial and abortive in point of theory, it is utterly poverty-stricken as respects ability to satisfy man's deeper needs. "He who thinks things out to their logical issue will find that naturalism leads nowhere: he will find himself driven to negation and despair. It is only through the intensity of her opposition to what she holds to be superstitious and illusory that naturalism herself can be deceived as to her own emptiness and her lack of any spiritually productive power."[2]

As compared with naturalism, immanent idealism commands a degree of tolerance from Professor Eucken. According to this scheme the thought world and the sense world are not antithetic, but are related as elements or aspects of a single whole. "They are related to one another as reality

---

[1] Life's Basis and Life's Ideal, p. 114.
[2] The Meaning and the Value of Life, p. 32.

and appearance, as cause and effect, as animating and animated nature. The divine is not so much a power transcending the world as one permeating and living in it; not something specific outside of things, but their connection in a living unity."[1] This type of thought has had wide currency in recent times. But in respect of light and leading for the age it is quite decidedly wanting. In pursuance of its premise on an all-controlling emphatically immanent reason or life-power, it slurs over the darker phases in the actual system of things, and gravitates into a pantheism destructive of the proper concept of the divine. Its promise is illusory. It furnishes no basis of permanent satisfaction.

Eucken considers whether culture, or advancing civilization, can be expected to bring to human life the needful enrichment and uplift. His conclusion is

---

[1] Life's Basis and Life's Ideal, p. 15.

adverse. "The impersonal work of culture and civilization," he says, "threatens to become mechanical from its very center outwards. No growth of inner potency corresponds to the increase of work, and expansion by far outweighs concentration; man becomes more and more the slave of his work and a bundle of isolated accomplishments."[1]

The verdict of the Professor on the competency of socialistic programs, of whatever order, to work effectually toward an ideal stage of man's life is equally negative. In his view Socialism is greatly at fault in making the economic point of view so perfectly controlling, and in overlooking both the evil in man—which is beyond the cure of mere agreeable conditions—and the deep needs of his spiritual nature. "Even from the remotest times," he writes, "there have been theorists who expected a complete social regeneration to ensue from the abolition and

---
[1] The Truth of Religion, pp. 58, 59.

restriction of the divisions between classes. More than two thousand years ago Aristotle met them with the objection that the complication goes deeper than they think, that the worst crimes are not the result of need, but of wantonness and a 'greed for more,' and that even though a new social regime might remove or remedy certain defects, it would be sure to introduce or strengthen others."[1] Culture of the socialistic type, Eucken contends, is too much a matter of the surface. "This culture only throws man back unceasingly upon the merely human, and unmercifully holds him firmly fixed in it. It chains him to his own appearance and suppresses all tendencies toward depth. It knows nothing of life's consciousness of itself; it knows no inner problems, no definite development of the soul; it cannot acknowledge a common life of an

---

[1] The Problem of Human Life as Viewed by the Great Thinkers, p. 549.

inner kind, but must derive all from external relations. At the same time it excludes all understanding of the movement of universal history; for the chief content of this movement constitutes just those problems which Socialism regards as foolish delusions. To be sure, the striving after an inner independence of life has brought much error with it, and it may involve much that is problematical. But that a longing after such independence should arise at all and prove itself able to call forth so much endeavor sufficiently demonstrates that man is more than a mere being of society, more than a member of a social organism."[1] "Prosperity," it is stated in another connection, "a life of careless enjoyment, cannot possibly suffice to make us happy, for while we are slaying one foe—sorrow and need—another, perhaps a worse one, is arising— namely, blankness and boredom; nor is

---
[1] Life's Basis and Life's Ideal, p. 58.

it easy to see how a socialistic program can help us to fight it. In truth, all civilization which simply aims at fostering and furthering man's immediate interests bears the inevitable impress of barrenness and desolation."[1]

In making this adverse comment the philosopher does not intend, of course, to disparage efforts to ameliorate social conditions. His strictures fall only upon the assumption that enterprise of this sort is able by itself to lift man out of his impoverishment into the fullness and satisfaction of a normal life.

In like manner Eucken finds in what has been called the "gospel of work" no proper remedy for the spiritual poverty so largely characteristic of the age. He admits, indeed, that the plea for absorbing activity is in the right as against a one-sided subjectivity or withdrawal from the work of the modern world,[2] but he repudiates

---
[1] The Meaning and the Value of Life, p. 47.
[2] The Truth of Religion, p. 68.

the notion that mere work can meet the demand of the inner life. "When we take," he says, "an inside view of life we find that a life of mere bustling routine preponderates, that men struggle and boast and strive to outdo one another, that unlimited ambition and vanity are characteristic of individuals, that they are always running to and fro and pressing forward, and feverishly exerting all their powers. But throughout it all we come upon nothing that gives any real value to life, and nothing spiritually elevating. Hence we do not find any meaning or value in life, but in the end a single huge show in which culture is reduced to a burlesque. Anyone who thinks it all over, and reflects upon the difference between the enormous labor that has been expended and the accompanying gain to the essentials of life, must either be driven to complete negation and despair, or must seek new ways of guaranteeing a value to life and liberating man from the sway of the pettily human."[1] "For a time we can stifle thought in work, but we cannot indefinitely work on for work's sake only. Voltaire's recipe—to work, but to ask no reasons—would, if put into practice, degrade us to mere beasts of burden."[2]

III

The above sketches the negative side of Professor Eucken's teaching relative to the way of meeting the pressing demand of the age. When we inquire after his positive prescription for fulfilling that demand we find that he has formulated one, if not in detail, at least in general terms, and is prepared to commend it with great earnestness of conviction. Stated in brief, his prescription is the vital recognition of a supreme spiritual life (Geistes-Leben), at once above the

---

[1] The Life of the Spirit, p. 88.
[2] The Meaning and the Value of Life, pp. 22, 23.

world and in the world, and the serious, thoroughgoing response of the individual to the nature and requirements of that life.

The ground for affirming the actuality of this supreme spiritual life consists not so much in formal demonstration as in the demand for such a life to serve as a credible basis for a rational system, and to furnish a satisfactory explanation of the content of human experience. The following passages will serve to illustrate this point of view:

"The transformation of all reality into a stream of becoming—provided we follow it to the bitter end, and do not stop arbitrarily in the middle— destroys all truth and empties life of all its content. Reality itself seems nothing more than an ephemeral world of shadows. Truth, in any and every meaning of the word, is possible only in contradistinction to the limitations and fluctuations of time. If we have nothing that we can oppose to time, then man and man's opinions are the sole arbiter of what we are to look upon as good and true. There is no longer any standard which will afford a measure of his capacity and act as a check on arbitrary caprice."[1] "We could not speak at all of truth over against mere opinion, or of good over against mere utility, unless there is some point of departure from the limits of mere humanity, and unless there is an acknowledgment of truth beyond man himself."[2] "The assertion of an independent spiritual life, transcendent over all human undertaking, is a sufficient safeguard against a destructive relativism."[3] "It is to be borne in mind that the spiritual life in man could never rise against the power of nature if it were no more than a purely human thing. Nature surrounds us a boundless kingdom of

---

[1] Christianity and the New Idealism, p. 41.
[2] The Truth of Religion, p. 512.
[3] Life's Basis and Life's Ideal, p. 224.

energies and laws; it surrounds us, not merely from without, but strikes deep into our own soul with thousandfold incessant effects. How could the spiritual life, which finds itself first in our aspiration, in any manner enforce its way against all this did we not stand upon inward connections, and had there not worked in us over against that which is given in the surrounding world the energy of a new kind of world?"[1] "Without the presence of the Infinite there would be no striving after truth, no energy for the good or for love over against egotistic utility."[2] In a word, the supreme spiritual life is a needed basis of any trustworthy system of truth, and it evidences itself by results wrought in the human spirit.

In describing the characteristics of the supreme spiritual life Professor Eucken emphasizes in particular its

---

[1] The Truth of Religion, pp. 159, 160.
[2] Ibid., p. 507.

independence, its transcendence of time limitations, and its immanence in the world process and especially in the life of humanity. The first of these points is very emphatically asserted, as appears in these specimen sayings: "To regard the spiritual life as merely man's work is to destroy it at the root. It cannot be understood save as a development of the organized universe, a development which takes place in man, communicates itself to man, but is never merely man's production."[1] "One thing we must, above all, bear in mind—that if the invisible world is to have the requisite stability and breadth, it cannot be the mere object of our finite longing or any inference laboriously drawn from the conditions of our finite experience; it must be completely independent, and exist in its own right. And this is impossible unless we are to find in it not the mere further development of our given

---

[1] Christianity and the New Idealism, p. 10.

powers along certain special lines, but the underived totality of life and being."[1]

The character of the supreme spiritual life as timeless, while yet in most intimate relations with the time world, is thus expressed: "Religion will demand in a most decisive manner that time with all its change and caprice shall not pass judgment on the spiritual life, but that the latter shall judge concerning the valuable and the valueless of the things of time."[2] "History is only valuable as being the medium through which the eternal reveals itself, as being that whose whole existence is but a struggle for the eternal."[3] "History cannot become a struggle for the content of the spiritual life unless the main standard of life is laid beyond the bare results of the times in a timeless order."[4] "The characteristic mark of the eternal is not a ca-

---
[1] The Meaning and the Value of Life, p. 75.
[2] The Truth of Religion, pp. 472, 473.
[3] Christianity and the New Idealism, p. 47.
[4] The Truth of Religion, p. 175.

pacity to maintain itself consistently unchanged amid all the changes of time. It is, rather, the ability to enter into the varied life of different epochs without losing itself in them, to manifest in them all its transcendent power, to pursue in them all the same end of freeing time from its purely temporal character."[1]

In the passage just cited the aspect of immanence is combined with that of eternity. Enforcement of the former aspect is contained also in sentences like these: "The divine is to us not only a world-transcendent sovereignty, but also a world-pervading power: to honor the former preponderantly may be the only salvation for times and individuals in a state of prostration and collapse, but this form of life can never be accepted as the normal one, and the one alone worth striving for."[2] "However certain it

---

[1] Christianity and the New Idealism, p. 65.
[2] Life's Basis and Life's Ideal, pp. 281, 282.

be that the basis of man's work must be laid within a spiritual Over-life, yet the precise form which it takes must be determined by his own struggle."[1] "The freedom and the self-activity of man are not a withdrawal of the divine power and the lessening of divine grace, but they are the verification of them—the highest verification of all."[2]

In Eucken's exposition of the supreme spiritual life it is easy to detect a kinship with the trend of the great idealistic philosophies. Professor Troeltsch has remarked: "In Eucken we have a combination of Plato, Fichte, and Hegel."[3] This statement we are inclined to regard as pretty well grounded. The transcendent independent spiritual life postulated by Eucken has a distinct kinship with the eternal ideas of Plato which serve as the rational and formative principle in

---
[1] The Meaning and the Value of Life, p. 98.
[2] The Truth of Religion, p. 223.
[3] The Harvard Review, October, 1912.

the world. Fichte's stress upon the moral order as immanent in reality and upon the subordination of nature to the personal agent has a noticeable, if not a complete, counterpart in Eucken's teaching. In Hegel's evolving thought as constitutive of the universe there is somewhat of a parallel to the supreme spiritual life which Eucken represents as leading on the development of the world. It should not be overlooked, however, that in stressing the transcendence as well as the immanence of the fundamental life principle the later philosopher stands in contrast with the great idealist of the preceding century.

In choosing "life" rather than "idea" or "thought" to give expression to the basal reality, the present-day philosopher was doubtless moved by the breadth of significance belonging to the first of these terms, as covering more than the purely intellectual, and as carrying suggestions of dynamic efficiency. Translated into the customary language of religion, the supreme spiritual life would appear to be none other than God. Indeed, Eucken says of the latter term: "It signifies nothing other than absolute spiritual life in its grandeur above all the limitations of man and the world of experience—a spiritual life that has attained to a complete subsistence in itself, and, at the same time, to an encompassing of all reality."

In this statement there is a recognition of that double aspect of transcendence and immanence which has been asserted to be characteristic of the supreme spiritual life. The same aspect is brought out very cogently in the following sentence: "The Godhead appears, on the one side, at an infinite height and distance above man, so that man discovers his pettiness with great bitterness; and, on the other side, the divine appears as most inti-

---

[1] The Truth of Religion, pp. 208, 209.

mate and as the dearest possession, so that man is raised through this to immeasurable greatness."[1] Thus the independent yet immanent *life* is identified with the *God* who is at once transcendent and immanent.

That Eucken uses the impersonal term prevailingly does not import, we judge, that he was ill-affected toward the conception of the divine personality. He asserts, in fact, that this conception within the life-process of religion is indispensable;[2] and it is natural to suppose that he rates a demand which is evolved in that process as correspondent to essential truth. It is to be noticed also that in his apparently commendatory reference to Professor Bowne's emphasis on the personal nature of the unifying principle which is back of the world constituents, he leaves it to be inferred that he postulates divine personality.[3]

---

[1] The Truth of Religion, p. 431.
[2] Ibid., p. 430.
[3] Zion's Herald, December 18, 1912.

Doubtless it is true that he gives evidence of a rather lively apprehension that the personality of God may be construed in a too anthropomorphic fashion. Equally it is not to be denied that one will fail to find in his books such a measure of explicit emphasis on the personality of God as is contained in the writings of Professor Bowne. Nevertheless, we infer that his conviction respecting the fact of divine personality was in line with that advocated by our own metaphysician.

IV

From the nature and function ascribed to the supreme spiritual life the office of religion is readily inferred. It serves as a practical means of connection with this transcendent reality, in union with which man is lifted out of all unworthy subjection to the time and sense world. To use the language of our philosopher: "Religion has opened out an intimate relationship with an infinite and absolute life, and has given our life an originality over against all attempts to classify it with the *causal nexus*. As religion thus places man between the two worlds, it calls him to a self-decision and makes freedom for the first time possible, for freedom remains an empty delusion as long as we are only pieces of a merely 'given' world. And for the first time religion furnishes the possibility of an inner renewal and of a new beginning through a contact with an inexhaustible depth."[1]

As respects the historical religions, Professor Eucken refuses to identify any one of them, in its actual form, with the absolute religion. The most that he concedes to Christianity is that it comes nearer to being an embodiment of the absolute religion than any other system of religious faith and practice. His words are: "As

---
[1] The Truth of Religion, p. 509.

certainly as there is only one sole truth, there can be only one absolute religion, and this religion coincides entirely in no way with any one of the historical religions. For they all conceive the divine under the conditions of the human situation; originating and growing in particular epochs, they have all to pay tribute to the characteristics and culture of such epochs. . . . The whole of our investigation leaves no doubt as to our position in regard to Christianity. A double aspect has already been fully noticed. On the one hand, Christianity in the nature of its substance appears as the highest embodiment of the absolute religion; and, on the other hand, a fundamental revision of its traditional existential form has become absolutely necessary."[1]

The relative superiority of Christianity is asserted by Eucken with unhesitating conviction. He notices, in

---

[1] The Truth of Religion, pp. 535, 539.

the first place, that it has a great advantage in the character of its personal center—a factor which is of great significance to any historical system. No unbiased mind, he maintains, can fail to acknowledge the unique preëminence of Jesus Christ. "Religion has here transformed itself into a human purity with wonderful energy and inwardness; an overtowering height has joined itself with a simple innocence; manly energy of action has united with gentle feelings, and a youthful joy of disposition with a deep discovery of suffering. . . . The personality of the Founder has thus become incomparably more to Christianity than the founders of all the other religions have become to their adherents."[1] "That life of Jesus exercises ever more a tribunal over the world; and the majesty of such an effective bar of judgment supersedes all the developments of external

---
[1] The Truth of Religion, pp. 16, 17.

power."[1] Other tributes equally appreciative might be cited.[2] It is worthy of notice also that the philosopher holds that historical criticism can never dim the image of Jesus which shines forth from the Gospels. It approves itself irresistibly as a copy of reality. "In the innermost traits of his being Jesus is more transparent and familiar to us than any hero of the world's history."[3]

Other points in the preëminence of Christianity are represented as corresponding in no small degree to the superlative worth of the Founder. For instance, Christianity, as no other religion, places love at the center, and exalts it as the controlling world-renewing power.[4] It begets a warm interest in all humanity, a longing to redeem every individual.[5] Again,

---
[1] The Truth of Religion, p. 361.
[2] See in particular The Problem of Human Life as Viewed by the Great Thinkers, pp. 169, 170.
[3] The Problem of Human Life as Viewed by the Great Thinkers, p. 151.
[4] Christianity and the New Idealism, pp. 136, 137.
[5] The Truth of Religion, p. 545.

Christianity by the power inherent in itself works for the transformation of the whole man.[1] Avoiding all shallow optimism, frankly recognizing man's deep estrangement from the right, it summons to a fundamental regeneration.[2] Once more Christianity makes close connection with an invisible world. And it does this without running into an ascetic disparagement of the present world. "For the fundamentally ethical character of Christianity causes its spiritual superiority to the world to become at the same time constructive of a higher world."[3]

V

As was brought out in one of the cited passages, Eucken is disposed to

---

[1] The Truth of Religion, pp. 495, 496.

[2] Christianity and the New Idealism, pp. 137–141. These pages may intimate that Eucken is not tied to a technical theory of original sin; but they certainly make plain, as also do statements in other connections, that he takes no rose-colored view of the actual moral tendencies and condition of men.

[3] The Problem of Human Life as Viewed by the Great Thinkers, p. 134.

unite with a profound appreciation of the lofty traits of Christianity an imperative demand for the reconstruction of its existential form. That in putting forward this demand he does not run into sheer arbitrariness will hardly be questioned by one who makes an unbiased study of the forms which Christianity has taken on in the course of the historical evolution. But to say this much is far from granting that Eucken himself has furnished, even in outline, a satisfactory doctrinal structure. Indeed, it is our conviction that, while a great part of his thought respecting the ideal Christian system is true and normal, he comes short on the person and work of Christ. So far as we have been able to discover, he does not accept even the essential feature of the catholic Christology. He greatly emphasizes, it is true, the union of the human and the divine as a most potent and salutary feature in Christian teaching. He criticizes, furthermore, a rationalistic paring down of the significance of Christ. But, after all, the plain import of his brief references to the subject of Christology is that he recognizes no transcendent sonship in Christ, and accords to him divinity only in the sense in which the exceptional man has divinity.[1] If he had more divinity than others, it was only because he more truly represented the human ideal than others.

A rejection of the proper divinity of Christ involves logically a like treatment of the doctrine of the Trinity. Eucken says but little on this theme, yet enough to indicate his negative attitude.

A very obvious comment on the Professor's revised Christology is, that it brings us face to face with a great

---

[1] The Truth of Religion, pp. 20, 206, 584, 585; The Problem of Life as Viewed by the Great Thinkers, pp. 151, 152; Christianity and the New Idealism, pp. 64, 80, 87, 120, 121; Life's Basis and Life's Ideal, p. 332.

practical difficulty. It collides with the New Testament—not merely with isolated passages in the New Testament, but with the trend of the New Testament as a whole. All the Gospels and nearly all of the Epistles make Christ distinctly more than a purely human ideal. To deny then his transcendent sonship goes so far in contradicting the primitive oracles of Christianity as seriously to assail its historical foundations. And thus to retrench historical foundations is not of slight consequence. Just in proportion as that is done the effective practical basis of Christianity is cut away, and it is left to swing in the mid-air of theoretical conceptions. Theoretical ideals may be well shaped and measurably edifying, but they are no substitute for a firm historical basis. As Eucken himself has said: "To construct a religion out of concepts cunningly strung together, what is it but to attempt to make a real material body out of phantoms?"[1] We distrust, accordingly, the religious outcome of any scheme which would dislodge the element of the transcendent sonship of Christ from the New Testament. That element is too closely interwoven with the fiber of the New Testament teaching to be taken out without injury to faith in the historical basis of Christianity.

Professor Eucken would doubtless contend, as indeed he has done, that the pure human ideal of Christ is self-attesting. But where is the warrant for asserting that the divine-human ideal as reflected in the New Testament is not self-attesting? Many close students have been profoundly convinced that it is of that nature. As one of them remarks in substance: "The harmony of the character of Christ as delineated in the Gospels, the intermingling of the divine and the human in such a way that the

---

[1] Christianity and the New Idealism, pp. 146, 147.

lowly and human never degrade him in our eyes, nor his power and greatness remove him out of our sympathies and understanding, is inconsistent with the supposition that the record as a source of historic truth has been impaired by theological bias. That such a picture was or could have been the growth of unconscious theologizing is far more incredible than that it is what it professes to be, the record of a sublime reality."[1] All through the Christian ages a very large proportion of those who have partaken most deeply of the life and power of Christianity have gained the same impression of the delineation of the divine-human Christ in the New Testament. If this ideal is to be vanquished by any doctrinaire construction, what is to guarantee that a like order of construction may not insist on paring down the purely hu-

---

[1] Somerville, Saint Paul's Conception of Christianity, pp. 225, 226.

man ideal? No, it is a serious matter to revise the New Testament Christology to the extent proposed. A critical surgery skillful enough to cut out the higher view of Christ without impairing the ground of confidence in the historic basis of Christianity is in no way likely to appear.

Furthermore, it is legitimate to contend that there is a loss of majesty and authority in making the incarnation, in relation to Christ, nothing more than a superior specimen of that union between the human and the divine which occurs in mankind generally. On the catholic theory of the incarnation of the eternal Son of God, Christianity at once takes rank as being in essential character the absolute religion. On the humanitarian theory of Eucken its right to such rank is open to question, and the inevitable tendency will be for it to recede from the masterful and commanding position which accrues to it in catholic teaching. Had the criticism of our philosopher been aimed against the artificial and overwrought Christological construction which has sometimes been obtruded on the faith of Christians, it would not be subject to challenge. But as being directed against any and every form of the catholic doctrine of the incarnation, we can but regard it as mistaken.

The like remark applies to Eucken's radical disparagement of the catholic conception of Christ's mediation. Not a little of the doctrinal construction on this theme, it may be admitted, has been one-sided and might very well be set aside. But that does not justify the summary exclusion of the idea of mediation, or the limitation of it simply to such manifestation of divine truth as may be furnished through a pure human subject. To reduce Christ's mediation to this measure, as Eucken evidently is minded to do,[1] is in emphatic contrast with the New Testament content and with the general trend of Christian thought and feeling through the centuries. The consistent carrying out of such a point of view would strip the hymn books of all the great historic communions of nearly half their contents. And what would be gained? An increased sense of the nearness of God? a more vivid realization of immediate relation with him? Rather, we believe, the opposite result would be likely to follow. Mediation, it is true, may be construed in a deistic sense, and so be accessory to placing God afar off, but there is no necessity of construing it in that sense. God is not afar off from the little child because in so large a degree he mediates his benevolence through the mother's smile, the mother's soothing touch, and all the watchcare of the mother in ward-

---

[1] The Truth of Religion, pp. 587, 589; Christianity and the New Idealism, pp. 120, 121.

ing off dangers and providing suitable means of nurture. The divine nearness is simply made concrete and effectual by the maternal ministry. And so throughout the whole ministry of man to man in any discretely ordered scheme. God is rather brought near to the apprehension of men, through the friendly service rendered to them by their fellows, than placed afar off.

Now the same God who employs the ministries of ordinary men to give ordinary expression to his good will may make use of the extraordinary ministry of a transcendent personality to give extraordinary expression to that good will. And if he should do so, he would in no wise sacrifice nearness or immediacy to mediation. He would simply give the most effective expression to his nearness. The well-beloved Son, the Christ, is mediator not as being set over against an absent God, but as giving ideal expression to a present God. He is perfectly qualified to be the mediator just because the perfect fullness of the Father dwells in him. Partaking without stint of the Father's will, purpose, life, he is able to reflect the perfect image of his love and righteousness. Perfect nearness and fullness of presence become the spring of perfect mediation. This is distinctly the New Testament view. The exalted sense of mediatorship or Saviourhood in the incarnate Son was always joined with an exalted sense of union with the Father. It was precisely because he was able to say, "The Father is in me and I am in the Father," that he could also claim with full confidence to be in an extraordinary sense a medium of blessing to men. His presence among men and his work for men emphasize the presence of the Father, insomuch that he is qualified to say, "He that hath seen me hath seen the Father." To the philosopher possibly his philosophic conception of the Divine may suffice, but to the common heart of humanity it is no substitute for the manifestation of God in Christ.

VI

A SUBORDINATE occasion for questioning the teaching of our philosopher is found in his treatment of the usual arguments for the divine existence—the cosmological, the teleological, and that from human nature taken as a basis of scientific induction. He rates them as incompetent to fulfill their purpose, and the ground of so rating them he expresses in these terms: "We must not forget that no province can prove anything outside its own reach, and that an attempt to do this leads into anthropomorphism."[1]

In so far as this proposition is meant to emphasize the truth that religion has evidences of peculiar effi-

---
[1] The Truth of Religion, pp. 513, 514.

cacy in its own worthful content, and is not in any complete sense dependent upon the data of scientific study, it is to be cordially approved. But it is possible to make too emphatic an antithesis between the scientific and the religious, an antithesis working to the disadvantage of religion itself. Indeed, we do not see how the assumption of such disparate spheres between the two as is contained in the cited proposition and in its application in the context can be maintained without prejudicial results. The universe certainly is not made up of watertight compartments. Eucken would not so claim. The supposition of the rationality of the world system—a supposition absolutely necessary to any security in intellectual procedure—implies a degree of correspondence between part and part. From any different point of view we are left inclosed by the limitations of the human province; and nothing can help us out. Not even the function of a supreme spiritual life can afford us an outlet, for we have no immediate knowledge of this transcendent reality. What we know immediately is certain effects in us which serve as a ground of rational inference—an inference none the less actual because possibly very swift and confident. These effects or experiences are data in a human province, and consequently, cannot give valid suggestions as to what is to be found in a higher province, if evidence cannot lead out of one province into another.

On this premise we seem to be consigned to the agnosticism which bars out all inquiry as to what is above and beyond. But agnosticism of this sort is discredited as being in the long run an impracticable and an intolerable alternative. Casting aside this alternative, we take the sane and warrantable course in appealing to the rationality of the universe as involving a degree of correspondence between part and part, and so providing that data in one department may have more or less significance for another province.

We conclude, then, that Eucken's proposition does not afford a well-grounded basis for his negative attitude toward the historic arguments for the divine existence. We are aware that the Professor is not without company in the position which he takes, and we appreciate his motive, namely, the wish to give due credit to the deliverances of the religious consciousness. We think, however, that he underrates the theistic proof which is afforded by a well-conducted attempt rationally to construe the world and man. As between Eucken and Bowne on the point in question, it strikes us that the latter is distinctly to be preferred.

In referring to one other point in Professor Eucken's thinking we are influenced less by an unequivocal occasion for criticism than by a desire to clarify, in some degree, the bearings or apologetic connections of a subject which is frequently brought to view in our time. The point concerns the estimate of miracles, and especially of the resurrection of Jesus. Now, we have not discovered that the Professor has any special ambition to launch out into a negative dogmatism on this theme. He stands, in fact, in contrast with some of our contemporaries, with their flippant ukase against miracles of all sorts. "With good reason," he says, "did our greatest poet call miracle the dearest child of faith. A religion entirely void of it is a self-contradiction."[1] He speaks, moreover, of the "miraculous transforming character of the entry of the divine into the human."[2] Miracle, then, he recognizes. The only question is as to the sphere in which he supposes it to be operative. Evidently, the sphere

---

[1] Christianity and the New Idealism, pp. 35, 36.
[2] Ibid., p. 80.

in which he prefers to find it is that of the working of a superhuman and supernatural life for the inner transformation of men. If he does not challenge outright the physical miracle, he rates it as no essential in the Christian religion. This is manifest from the tone of his comment on the miracle most distinctly emphasized in the New Testament, the resurrection of Jesus. Faith in the bodily resurrection he declares is no necessity for religion. "Faith has as its object what is of a timeless nature—what is able to be immediately present to each individual and able to manifest its own elevating energy."[1] In weighing this declaration the pertinent consideration, it seems to us, lies in a discrimination between what is strictly necessary for the individual and what is necessary for the efficient fulfillment of a distinct historical vocation in a given world by a religion. An indi-

---

[1] The Truth of Religion, pp. 552, 553.

vidual may undoubtedly enter into the reality of the spiritual life without having embraced the bodily resurrection of Jesus as an object of faith. But does that prove that the historic truth of the resurrection is a matter of indifference to religion? Far from it. Fervent faith in the resurrection of the Crucified One was like a vital breath from heaven to incipient Christianity. Nor has it been of slight efficacy in later times. It has served as a great factor in giving to the Christian religion tangibility, reality, and power to grip the souls of men.

In general, a religion armed with victorious power needs to incorporate truth and set it forth in apprehensible form. It must be on good terms with the concrete. It must furnish intelligible tokens that God has actually wrought something in behalf of men and in demonstration of his interest. In proportion as religion leaves truth in an abstract range it is curtailed in the power of effective appeal. An abstract religion, as was intimated in a previous connection, is simply disqualified for world conquest in any large sense. In this view it becomes no light matter to cut out the resurrection and the other miracles associated with Jesus. They are congenially related to his exceptional person and office. They enter as a congruous factor into a great New Testament complex. To tear them out of that complex must have a serious bearing upon the historic basis of Christianity. It makes a longer step than some in our day imagine toward reducing Christianity to the weakened and impoverished condition of an abstract religion, a group of conceptions without certified historical setting or guaranteed basis in objective reality.

VII

PROFESSOR EUCKEN, in our view, is performing a substantial service to this generation in emphasizing the truth that religion is indispensable to depth and fullness of life and to permanent satisfaction in life. He also earns grateful appreciation by his inculcation of the truth that religion in its proper character lives in a vital recognition of and participation in a transcendent life, the unchanging source and standard of all goodness and truth. We only regret that in dealing with historical Christianity he should have thought it necessary to exscind certain cardinal points of view which are deeply imbedded in New Testament teaching, and which cannot be cut away without detriment at once to the historical basis of Christianity and to the completeness of its content.